KIDS ON EARTH

Wildlife Adventures – Explore The World

Euro Lynx

Sensei Paul David

COPYRIGHT PAGE

Kids On Earth: Wildlife Adventures - Explore The World

Euro Lynx

by Sensei Paul David,

Copyright © 2023.

All rights reserved.

978-1-77848-193-2 KoE_WildLife_Amazon_PaperbackBook_euro lynx

978-1-77848-192-5 KoE_WildLife_Amazon_eBook_euro lynx

978-1-77848-426-1 KoE_Wildlife_Ingram_Paperbackbook_EuroLynxCat Paperback

This book is not authorized for free distribution copying.

www.senseipublishing.com

@senseipublishing
#senseipublishing

Synopsis

In this book, we took a closer look at the unique and fascinating facts about the European Lynx. We explored its habitat and diet, its behavior and conservation efforts, and learned about its impressive abilities. We also discussed the threats that this species faces, and how we can help to protect them. We hope that this book has given you a greater appreciation for this beautiful animal, and that you will help to conserve and protect them in the years to come.

Get Our FREE Books Now!

kidsonearth.life

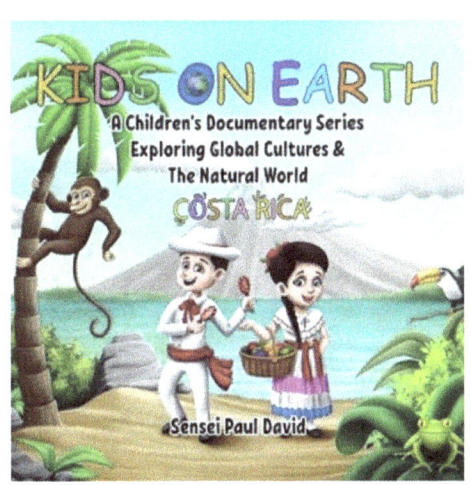

kidsonearth.world

Click Below for Another Book In Each Series

senseipublishing.com/KoE_SERIES

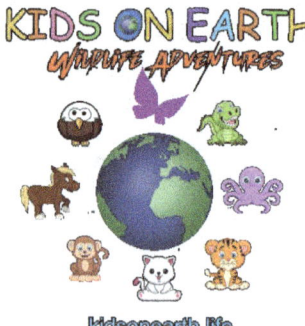

senseipublishing.com/KoE_Wildlife_SERIES

KoE En Español

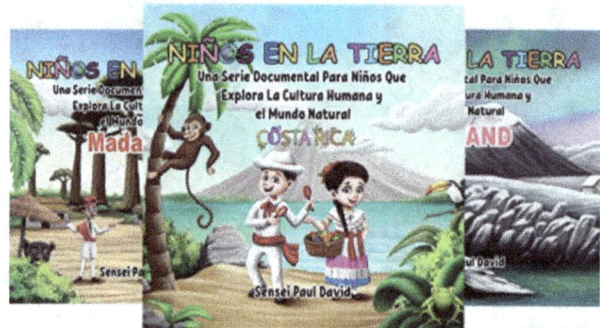

senseipublishing.com/KoE_SERIES_SPANISH

www.senseipublishing.com

Join Our Publishing Journey!

If you would like to receive FUTURE FREE BOOKS and get to know us better, please click www.senseipublishing.com and join our newsletter by entering your email address in the pop-up box.

Follow Our Blog: senseipauldavid.ca

Follow/Like/Subscribe: Facebook, Instagram, YouTube: @senseipublishing

Scan the QR Code with your phone or tablet to follow us on social media:

Like / Subscribe / Follow

Introduction

Welcome to the exciting world of the European Lynx! This beautiful, wildcat is the largest of its species in the world, and is found in many parts of Europe. In this book, we will explore the unique and fascinating facts about this incredible animal. From its habitat and diet, to its behavior and conservation efforts, we will take a closer look at these amazing creatures. So buckle up, and let's get started!

The European Lynx is the largest of the species, with males weighing up to 30 kilograms and females around half that size.

The European Lynx has a thick and silky fur coat that varies in color from yellow-brown to grayish-brown.

The European Lynx is a solitary animal, and they prefer to live alone.

This species of Lynx hunts by stalking and ambushing its prey.

The European Lynx has a diet that mainly consists of small mammals, such as hares, rabbits, and rodents.

The European Lynx can live up to 10 years in the wild.

The European Lynx is an excellent climber, and can often be seen perched in the branches of trees.

The European Lynx has a unique vocalization that sounds like a low-pitched purr.

The European Lynx has a large range across Europe, and can be found in countries such as Germany, France, and Switzerland.

The European Lynx communicates with its kin by scent marking.

The European Lynx is an endangered species, and its numbers have been declining due to habitat loss and hunting.

The European Lynx has large, tufted ears that can rotate 180 degrees, helping them to detect prey from far away.

The European Lynx is a very shy animal, and will usually try to avoid humans.

The European Lynx has a wide range of vocalizations, including hisses, growls, and purrs.

The European Lynx is an opportunistic hunter, and will often feed on carrion if it can find it.

The European Lynx is an ambush predator, and it stalks its prey before pouncing.

The European Lynx typically lives in forested areas, such as coniferous and mixed woodland.

The European Lynx is a territorial animal, and will often mark its territory with urine or scent markings.

The European Lynx is an adaptable animal, and can survive in a wide range of habitats.

The European Lynx has a loud and distinctive call that can be heard from far away.

The European Lynx will often use its sharp claws to climb trees in order to escape predators.

The European Lynx has excellent night vision, which helps it to find and hunt prey in the dark.

The European Lynx is a nocturnal animal, and it usually hunts at night.

The European Lynx has a thick tail that helps it to balance and keep warm.

The European Lynx is a solitary hunter, and will usually hunt alone.

The European Lynx has long legs and a body that is well adapted to climbing and jumping.

The European Lynx is an ambush predator, and it will often wait in hiding before attacking its prey.

The European Lynx is an expert swimmer, and can often be seen swimming across rivers and lakes in search of food.

The European Lynx has an impressive sense of smell, which helps it to locate prey.

The European Lynx is a powerful predator, and can take down large prey such as deer and wild boar.

Conclusion

We hope you have enjoyed learning about the amazing European Lynx! This incredible animal is a powerful predator, and a skilled hunter. From its thick coat of fur to its impressive night vision, the European Lynx is an amazing creature. We hope that you have gained a greater appreciation for this beautiful species, and that you will help to conserve and protect them in the years to come.

Thank you for reading this book!

If you found this book helpful, I would be grateful if you would **post an honest review on Amazon** so this book can reach other supportive readers like you!

All you need to do is digitally flip to the back and leave your review. Or visit amazon.com/author/senseipauldavid click the correct book cover and click on the blue link next to the yellow stars that say, "customer reviews."

As always...

It's a great day to be alive!

Share Our FREE eBooks Now!

kidsonearth.life

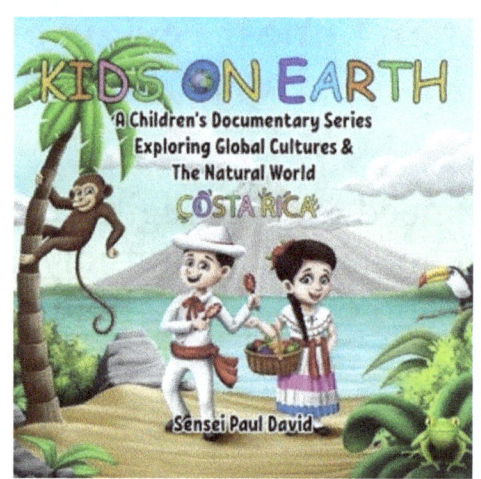

kidsonearth.world

Click Below for Another Book In Each Series

senseipublishing.com/KoE_SERIES

senseipublishing.com/KoE_Wildlife_SERIES

KoE En Español

senseipublishing.com/KoE_SERIES_SPANISH

www.senseipublishing.com

www.senseipublishing.com

@senseipublishing
#senseipublishing

Check out our **recommendations** for other books for adults & kids plus other great resources by visiting
www.senseipublishing.com/resources/

Join Our Publishing Journey!

If you would like to receive FREE BOOKS and special offers, please visit www.senseipublishing.com and join our newsletter by entering your email address in the pop-up box

Follow Our Engaging Blog NOW!
senseipauldavid.ca

Get Our FREE Books Today!

Click & Share the Links Below

FREE Kids Books
lifeofbailey.senseipublishing.com
kidsonearth.senseipublishing.com

FREE Self-Development Book

senseiselfdevelopment.senseipublishing.com

FREE BONUS!!!
Experience Over 25 FREE Engaging Guided Meditations!

Prized Skills & Practices for Adults & Kids. Help Restore Deep Sleep, Lower Stress, Improve Posture, Navigate Uncertainty & More.

Download the Free Insight Timer App and click the link below:
http://insig.ht/sensei_paul

About Sensei Publishing

Sensei Publishing commits itself to helping people of all ages transform into better versions of themselves by providing high-quality and research-based self-development books with an emphasis on mental health and guided meditations. Sensei Publishing offers well-written e-books, audiobooks, paperbacks, and online courses that simplify complicated but practical topics in line with its mission to inspire people toward positive transformation.

It's a great day to be alive!

About the Author

I create simple & transformative eBooks & Guided Meditations for Adults & Children proven to help navigate uncertainty, solve niche problems & bring families closer together.

I'm a former finance project manager, private pilot, jiu-jitsu instructor, musician & former University of Toronto Fitness Trainer. I prefer a science-based approach to focus on these & other areas in my life to stay humble & hungry to evolve. I hope you enjoy my work and I'd love to hear your feedback.

- It's a great day to be alive!
Sensei Paul David

Scan & Follow/Like/Subscribe: Facebook, Instagram, YouTube: @senseipublishing

Scan using your phone/iPad camera for Social Media
Visit us at www.senseipublishing.com and sign up for our newsletter to learn more about our exciting books and to experience our FREE Guided Meditations for Kids & Adults.

www.ingramcontent.com/pod-product-compliance
Lightning Source LLC
Chambersburg PA
CBHW080615110526
44587CB00040BB/3724